Making Things

Watch Me
Make a Mask

By Jack Otten

Welcome Books

Children's Press®
A Division of Scholastic Inc.
New York / Toronto / London / Auckland / Sydney
Mexico City / New Delhi / Hong Kong
Danbury, Connecticut

Photo Credits: Cover and all photos by Maura Boruchow
Contributing Editor: Jennifer Silate
Book Design: Michelle Innes

Library of Congress Cataloging-in-Publication Data

Otten, Jack.
Watch me make a mask / by Jack Otten.
   p. cm. -- (Making things)
  Includes index.
Summary: Shows a young boy turning a plain white mask into a monster face by using colored markers.
   ISBN 0-516-23944-9 (lib. bdg.) -- ISBN 0-516-23499-4 (pbk.)
   1. Mask making--Juvenile literature. [1. Mask making. 2. Handicraft.] I. Title.

TT898 .O88 2002
646.4'8--dc21

                      2001032343

Contents

My name is John.

I am going to a party tomorrow.

I am going to make a **mask** to wear.

5

I am going to make my mask look like a **monster.**

I will use red, green, and black **markers** to color my mask.

I use the red marker to color the eyes and the lips.

Red eyes make the mask look **scary**!

I color the rest of the mask with the green marker.

I carefully color around the eyes and the lips.

Now, I draw some hair.

The black marker covers the green.

13

Next, I draw eyebrows on the mask.

The eyebrows make the mask look **angry**!

15

There is a hole on each side of the mask.

I tie a piece of string to each hole.

I put the mask on my face.

I tie the pieces of string together.

The strings hold the mask in place.

19

My mask is finished.

Do I look scary?

21

New Words

angry (**ang**-gree) feeling hurt or mad

markers (**mar**-kuhrz) pens with colored ink

mask (**mask**) a face covering

monster (**mahn**-stuhr) a scary,
make-believe creature

scary (**scair**-ee) making someone feel
afraid

To Find Out More

Books
Crafty Masks
by Thomasina Smith
Gareth Stevens Audio

Cut and Make Indonesian Masks
by A.G. Smith
Dover Publications

Web Site
Masks
http://www.enchantedlearning.com/crafts/maskcrafts/
There are many fun mask-making projects on this Web site.

Index

About the Author
Jack Otten is an author and educator living in New York City.

Reading Consultants
Kris Flynn, Coordinator, Small School District Literacy, The San Diego County Office of Education

Shelly Forys, Certified Reading Recovery Specialist, W.J. Zahnow Elementary School, Waterloo, IL

Sue McAdams, Former President of the North Texas Reading Council of the IRA, and Early Literacy Consultant, Dallas, TX